DEPARTMENT OF HEALTH AND SOCIAL SECURITY

HOME OFFICE

WELSH OFFICE

LORD CHANCELLOR'S DEPARTMENT

Reform of Mental Health Legislation

Presented to Parliament by the Secretary of State for Social Services, the Secretary of State for the Home Department, the Secretary of State for Wales and the Lord Chancellor

by Command of Her Majesty

November 1981

LONDON

HER MAJESTY'S STATIONERY OFFICE

£2·65

Cmnd. 8405

ISBN 0 10 184050 0

CONTENTS

INTRODUCTION

1. The object of this White Paper is to explain the changes proposed in the Mental Health (Amendment) Bill which the Government has presented to Parliament.

2. The 1959 Mental Health Act was introduced during Mr. Harold Macmillan's administration to implement the main proposals of the Royal Commission on the Law Relating to Mental Illness and Mental Deficiency about the *status* and *legal position* of mentally disordered people in society. In brief, the Act removed statutory control from the great majority of mentally disordered people and set out new conditions for the minority who still need to be subject to special control, whether for the protection of themselves or others. It also ensured that mentally disordered people could benefit from general health and social services facilities by providing that existing legislation (eg the National Health Service Act 1946 and the National Assistance Act 1948) should apply to them.

3. The 1959 Act has worked well. Its first object, to remove statutory control from most mentally disordered people, was achieved and it provided a balanced system for the protection and control of the remaining small minority. But after nearly twenty years, the need for some revision and updating—within the overall framework of the Act—became apparent. A Consultation Paper issued in 1976 was followed in 1978 by the previous Government's White Paper 'The Review of the Mental Health Act 1959' (Cmnd 7320). This White Paper was generally welcomed both by the health and social work professions and by other bodies and individuals concerned about the care of the mentally disordered. Since then detailed comments have been offered and further consultations have taken place. This Government's conclusions are embodied in the Bill they have presented.

4. The Government has made clear the high priority which it wishes health and local authorities to give to developing services for mentally ill and mentally handicapped people. It has done so both in its guidance to authorities 'Care in Action'[1] and in its recent discussion papers on resource distribution 'Care in the Community'.[2] This priority is not affected by the Bill. The Bill is about the status and legal position of those mentally disordered people who need special protection or control. It is not about the services for the much larger number of mentally ill and mentally handicapped people in hospital and in the community as a whole.

The Main Objects of the Bill

5. The Bill improves safeguards for detained patients, clarifies the position of staff looking after them and removes uncertainties in the law.

---

[1]'Care in Action' was published in England.
[2]'Care in the Community' was published in England and Wales.

6. The main improvements are set out below. The references in brackets are to passages explaining them in more detail in the text of this White Paper.

i. The period before detention has to be either renewed or ended is halved (para 19).

ii. For certain groups, detention in hospital is allowed *only* if the person is thought treatable (paras 13 and 20).

iii. Access to Mental Health Review Tribunals is increased (paras 23–28).

iv. The position on consent to treatment is clarified (paras 35–40).

v. The standards of care given to detained patients and the use of powers of detention are safeguarded through the new Mental Health Act Commission (paras 29–34, 40).

vi. Guardianship powers are made to fit current good practice (paras 43–45).

vii. Increased opportunity for psychiatric assessment and treatment to be provided for those appearing before the courts by introducing, as resources allow, interim hospital orders and remands to hospital (paras 49–51).

CHAPTER 1

DEFINITION OF MENTAL DISORDER

7. The Mental Health Act 1959 sets out the forms of mental disorder which are covered by its provisions. These are mental illness, severe subnormality, psychopathic disorder and subnormality.

Mental Handicap

8. The Government shares the concern which is widely felt that mental handicap should not be confused with mental illness and that the needs of different groups of people should be recognised. They have also considered with the greatest care whether it is still appropriate to provide compulsory powers in respect of any mentally handicapped people and, if so, how this should be done.

9. The weight of professional opinion is that there is a very small minority of mentally handicapped people, without any other mental disorder, who do need to be detained in hospital—usually for their own safety. The Government recognises the importance of stressing that this is only a small minority. While, therefore, the Bill continues to provide for the compulsory detention which is required, subject to all the safeguards provided, in these cases, it does make a change in the words used. 'Severe subnormality' and 'subnormality' are to be replaced by the more up to date terms 'severe mental handicap' and 'mental handicap'.

10. The Government has decided it is not practicable to have entirely separate legislation for mentally handicapped people. It would be helpful, though, to separate out the provisions of mental health legislation which apply to mentally handicapped people. For technical reasons it would be cumbersome to do this during the passage of an amending Bill. References to mental handicap and severe mental handicap appear alongside references to the other disorders, in numerous places in the 1959 Act; to delete these references and bring them together in a separate Part of the Act by means of amending legislation would produce a very long and complex Bill. It would be almost impossible for practitioners in the field who have to implement the amended legislation to find their way through it. The Government therefore intends to present a consolidation of mental health legislation to Parliament soon after the present Bill is passed. The consolidated Mental Health Act will set out separately the provisions of the legislation which need to apply to mentally handicapped people.

Mental Illness

11. Mental illness is not further defined and no change is proposed. This condition accounts for the majority of the persons detained in hospital under the Act—some 5,000 of the 7,000 detained patients. As in the case of mental handicap, it is important to understand that the powers required for the small proportion of mentally ill people who need to be detained—7% of the mentally ill in hospital—do not have any implications for the treatment and care of the remainder of those suffering from mental illness.

Psychopathic Disorder

12. The Government has considered whether psychopathic disorder should be excluded from the Act, bearing in mind the discussion in the Butler Report on Mentally Abnormal Offenders (Cmnd 6244). The weight of current medical opinion is that most psychopaths are not likely to benefit from treatment in hospital and are for the penal system to deal with when they do commit offences but that there are some persons suffering from psychopathic disorder who can be helped by detention in hospital. For this reason, this category is not excluded from the Act.

Age Limits

13. At present, one of the limitations on compulsory admission powers is that they can only be applied to mentally subnormal and psychopathic patients if they are under 21 (although once admitted, the patients can continue to be detained after the age of 25 if they are considered dangerous, under section 44 of the Act). The origin of the age limit lay in medical opinion that mentally handicapped or psychopathic adults were unlikely to benefit from hospital treatment. In the Government's view, this age limit has been shown in the light of recent medical knowledge to be arbitrary. Moreover, it does not apply when courts make hospital orders on mentally disordered offenders and so makes an unnecessarily sharp distinction between those detained under civil powers (Part IV of the Act) and those who have been tried for an offence (Part V). It seems more reasonable to replace the age limit with a provision that would allow mentally handicapped and psychopathic patients of any age to be detained but only if there are grounds for believing that they are likely to benefit from medical treatment (see para 20). This criterion will replace the reference to "requires or is susceptible to medical treatment" in the definition of these forms of mental disorder. The interpretation of medical treatment in the context of the Act will be amended, in keeping with developments since 1959, to include habilitation and rehabilitation instead of training.

CHAPTER 2

COMPULSORY ADMISSION TO HOSPITAL

14. There are a number of different powers under which a patient may be compulsorily detained in hospital:

section 29 of the 1959 Act authorises admission for up to 3 days in an emergency;

section 25 authorises detention for 28 days for observation;

section 26 is a longer-term power to detain patients for treatment (subject to renewal—see paragraph 19);

section 30 gives doctors the power in an emergency to prevent informal patients from leaving hospital for up to 3 days;

section 136 gives the police the power to bring to hospital or a place of safety a patient found in a public place who seems to be mentally disordered and in need of immediate care or control.

In addition:

under section 60 mentally disordered offenders may be made subject to a hospital order by a court; and

under sections 72 and 73 prisoners may be transferred to hospital by the Home Secretary.

The Bill proposes some changes to most of these powers to ensure that patients are detained for no longer than necessary and to improve the working of the Act.

Social Workers undertaking Duties under the Act

15. One proposal in the Bill is relevant to most of the admission powers. In the 1959 Act the "mental welfare officer" plays a key role in considering compulsory admission to hospital (though applications for admission may also be made by the patient's nearest relative, or any relative in emergency). Since 1959, local authorities social services departments have been established and their functions greatly developed. The Bill provides that local authorities should "approve" social workers to carry out the functions of mental welfare officers. The arrangement would be in some ways similar to that under which health authorities approve doctors as having special experience in the diagnosis or treatment of mental disorder (section 28). Guidance on approval of social workers is being prepared in consultation with professional associations, training bodies, employing authorities and other interested organisations. The Bill also makes clear the role and function of the social worker and provides that he must interview the patient before he makes an application for admission to hospital and must satisfy himself that detention in hospital is the most appropriate means of ensuring that the patient receives the care and treatment he needs.

Emergency admissions

16. Section 29 provides a power to detain patients in emergencies and therefore involves a less formal procedure than section 25, which was intended as the normal admission power. In particular it requires the recommendation of only one doctor, who need not have any specialised psychiatric training, whereas section 25 requires two medical recommendations, one of which must be that of a doctor approved for the purpose under section 28. The Bill therefore proposes amendments to ensure that section 29 is only used in genuine emergencies. The person making the application must have seen the patient within the previous 24 hours, rather than 3 days as at present. The period of 3 days from completing the application, within which the patient must be admitted to hospital, is also to be reduced to 24 hours. The Bill also provides that the right to make an emergency application should be restricted to the patient's nearest relative (as well as a mental welfare officer) rather than any relative.

28 day power

17. The procedure set out in section 25 is referred to in the 1959 Act as admission for observation. Because of developments in psychiatry since the Act was passed it is now used also as a short-term treatment power. It is therefore felt that "assessment" is a more suitable term than "observation" as it implies more active intervention to form a diagnosis and plan treatment. In many cases compulsory detention need not extend beyond (or as long as) the 28 days which is the maximum period of detention under a section 25 application; the Bill therefore provides that patients detained under section 25 may be treated for their mental disorder without their consent where necessary in certain circumstances (consent to treatment is considered more fully in paras 35–40 below).

18. Such patients are afforded further protection in the Bill which proposes that it should be possible for the nearest relative of a patient detained under section 25 to discharge the patient, subject to the limitation in section 48 of the Act where the responsible medical officer considers the patient to be dangerous; at present this right applies only to patients detained under section 26. In addition, patients detained under section 25 will be able to apply to a Mental Health Review Tribunal for their detention to be reviewed. For practical reasons application must be made within the first 14 days of detention and the hearing will take place shortly afterwards. For these short-term cases the Tribunal will of necessity have to evolve new arrangements and will usually have to rely largely on the medical and social workers' reports made at the time of admission, with perhaps an oral report from the patient's responsible medical officer. It will nonetheless provide a new and worthwhile safeguard for patients detained under section 25.

Longer-term powers

19. The longer-term power of detention under section 26 will be amended to remove the age limits and include the "treatability" test described in para 20. In addition the duration of authority to detain a patient under section 26. will be reduced from one year to 6 months in the first instance. This would be

renewable on the first occasion for a further 6 months (compared with first renewal for a year now) and subsequently for a year at a time (instead of for 2 years at a time now). In other words the period of detention, before renewal has to be considered, will in all these cases be halved. Patients will consequently have more opportunities to apply to a Mental Health Review Tribunal (see para. 24 and Table 1). The Bill also proposes that the responsible medical officer should be specifically required to satisfy himself on renewal of detention that the patient is still suffering from mental disorder for which medical treatment in a hospital is appropriate and that the treatment cannot be provided unless detention continues.

Treatability

20. The Mental Health (Amendment) Bill provides that the "treatability" test—whether treatment is likely to alleviate or prevent a deterioration in the patient's condition—will in future apply to all patients when their detention is renewed. Detention will not be renewed unless there is an expectation of further benefit from treatment, except in the case of the mentally ill and severely mentally handicapped. Here the Bill recognises that the health services have a responsibility to care for mentally ill and severely mentally handicapped people whose disorder may make them unable to care for themselves by providing that even if the treatability test is not met, detention can still be renewed if the patient is unlikely to be able to care for himself, to obtain the care which he needs or guard himself against serious exploitation.

Patients already in hospital

21. Section 30 is concerned with patients who are already being treated in hospital as informal patients. Such a patient may be detained for up to 3 days if this seems necessary to the doctor in charge of the patient's treatment. This power is used when, for example, an informal patient wishes to leave hospital and the doctor in charge believes that the conditions for compulsory detention are satisfied but has not time to complete the full application procedure (which involves a mental welfare officer or the patient's nearest relative). Nurses have sometimes found it difficult in an emergency to contact immediately the doctor in charge of the patient's treatment so that the detention power can be exercised and have been uncertain about their legal position in trying to prevent a patient from leaving when it is clearly best that he should not.

22. The Bill therefore includes changes which will help to ensure that mentally disordered patients receive the treatment they need and which will put beyond doubt the legal position of the staff concerned. Firstly, it will be possible for the power of detention to be exercised by any doctor on the staff of the hospital who is nominated by the doctor in charge of the patient's treatment to act for him in his absence. Secondly, a registered mental nurse or registered nurse for the mentally subnormal will be able to invoke a holding power until the arrival of a doctor with the power to detain the patient; the holding power will in any case lapse after 6 hours. It will apply only where a patient is already under medical treatment for mental disorder. If the nurse decides to exercise the holding power he or she must record, in writing, his or her judgment that the patient is suffering from mental disorder to such a

degree that it is necessary in the interests of the patient's health or safety or for the protection of others for him to be immediately restrained from leaving the hospital and that it is not practicable to ensure the immediate attendance of a doctor empowered to detain the patient. As soon as this has been recorded the holding power takes effect. The nurse must give the record to the hospital managers (or whoever is acting for them) as soon as possible.

CHAPTER 3

SAFEGUARDS FOR PATIENTS AND STAFF

Mental Health Review Tribunals

23. The Bill gives patients more opportunities to apply to a Mental Health Review Tribunal. It will also introduce automatic Tribunal hearings for patients whose position has not been reviewed by a Tribunal for 3 years. Overall, it is thought that the number of Tribunal hearings will rise from 904 in 1980 to around 4,500 a year. The opportunity to have the need for continued detention reviewed by an independent body is an important safeguard and the Government believes that the proposed increase in the frequency of such reviews is a significant improvement, at no great cost.

24. As explained in paragraph 18 above, patients detained under section 25 (for 28 days) will have a right to apply to a Tribunal for an immediate review of their case. Patients detained under section 26, including unrestricted patients under hospital orders and unrestricted patients transferred from prison will have twice as many opportunities to apply to a Tribunal as a consequence of the periods of detention being halved. Restricted patients will be able to ask for a Tribunal hearing once in the second year of their detention and every year thereafter. In addition, the Bill proposes that hospital managers must refer to a Tribunal any patient who has been detained under section 26 but has not had a Tribunal hearing in the first 6 months of detention. A similar provision will apply to *unrestricted* patients detained under Part V of the Act. Hospital managers will also be required to refer to a Tribunal any patient who has been detained for 3 years without a Tribunal hearing. These proposals will ensure that patients who lack the ability or initiative to make an application to a Tribunal also have the safeguard of an independent review of their case.

25. Table 1 illustrates the changes for a patient who is detained first under section 25 then section 26. If he is detained continuously for 4 years he would have, under the present Act, only 3 opportunities to apply to a Tribunal. The Bill will provide 6 opportunities for the patient to apply to a Tribunal in his first 4 years of detention, with a minimum of 2 Tribunal hearings (after 7 months and 3 years 7 months) if he makes no application himself.

26. Patients under guardianship will also have more opportunities to apply to a Tribunal, in line with the shorter duration of each period of guardianship—6 months, 6 months, then a year at a time. They will not be covered by the arrangements for automatic reviews, since their liberty is not restricted in the same way as patients detained in hospital.

27. The Bill will also give detained patients under 16 years of age the right to apply to a Tribunal. In the 1959 Act patients under 16 have no such right, though if they are detained under Part V their nearest relative may apply to a Tribunal on their behalf. The Government considers it important that all

detained patients should have access to a Tribunal. Hospital managers are to be required to refer the very small number of patients under 16 for an automatic review at the end of any 12-month period in which they (or their nearest relative) have not made an application, rather than every 3 years as for adults.

28. Tribunals sometimes wish to ensure that suitable arrangements are made for the care of a patient before he is released. The Bill therefore provides them with the power to order delayed discharge. The Tribunal Rules are also being revised to provide more flexibility in the way cases are handled. The panels from which Tribunal members are chosen may be enlarged since there are to be many more Tribunal hearings, some of which (because of the improvements for patients admitted under section 25) may have to be arranged at very short notice.

TABLE 1: *Rights of Application to the Mental Health Review Tribunal (MHRT)*

	1959 ACT	1959 ACT AS AMENDED BY MENTAL HEALTH BILL
Month One	Admission under Section 25	Admission under Section 25 RIGHT OF APPLICATION TO MHRT IN FIRST 14 DAYS
Month Two	Detention for one year under Section 26 RIGHT OF APPLICATION TO MHRT BETWEEN MONTHS 2 AND 7	Detention for 6 months under Section 26 RIGHT OF APPLICATION TO MHRT BETWEEN MONTHS 2 AND 7
Month Eight		Detention renewed for 6 months AUTOMATIC REVIEW IF NO REVIEW SOUGHT IN MONTHS 2 TO 7 RIGHT OF APPLICATION TO MHRT BETWEEN MONTHS 8 AND 13
Month Thirteen	Detention renewed for one year RIGHT OF APPLICATION TO MHRT BETWEEN MONTHS 13 AND 24	Detention renewed for one year RIGHT OF APPLICATION TO MHRT BETWEEN MONTHS 13 AND 24
Month Twenty-five	Detention renewed for two years RIGHT OF APPLICATION TO MHRT BETWEEN MONTHS 25 AND 48	Detention renewed for one year RIGHT OF APPLICATION TO MHRT BETWEEN MONTHS 25 AND 36
Month Thirty-seven		Detention renewed for one year RIGHT OF APPLICATION TO MHRT BETWEEN MONTHS 37 AND 48
Month Forty-four		AUTOMATIC REVIEW IF NO REVIEW SOUGHT SINCE MONTH 8

Mental Health Act Commission

29. The most important safeguards to ensure that patients are not detained unnecessarily are the carefully drawn criteria for admission and renewal of detention and access to Mental Health Review Tribunals; but other checks are also needed. The 1978 White Paper discussed the possibility of setting up mental welfare commissions on the lines of the Scottish Mental Welfare Commission, to protect psychiatric patients, but concluded that it was wrong in principle to reintroduce a system for psychiatric patients which was fundamentally different from that for other patients. The present Government takes a

different view: patients detained under the compulsory powers of the Mental Health Act are in a unique position because they have no right to discharge themselves, unlike all other patients including other psychiatric patients. It is essential to ensure therefore that the procedures leading to the detention of such patients and the renewal of the authority for their detention are subject to scrutiny. The responsibility for undertaking this scrutiny must rest with a body which is independent of those who have been involved in the compulsory admission and continued detention. Accordingly the Government proposes to set up a Mental Health Act Commission with a general protective function for detained patients.

30. A new factor since 1978 which has further influenced the Government on this matter is one of the proposals made by the Rampton Hospital Management Review Team, chaired by Sir John Boynton, which reported to the Secretary of State in October 1980 on the management of Rampton Special Hospital. In considering the wider issues surrounding their enquiry the Review Team said:

> "There is a strong case for an appointed body to inspect and monitor closed institutions such as Rampton and the other special hospitals, or indeed wherever patients are subject to detention under the Mental Health Act. The exact powers and functions of such a body would be for further consideration, but we think it might be constituted on the lines of the old Board of Control or the Scottish Mental Welfare Commission. Its functions might include the review of patient care and treatment, the independent investigation of more serious complaints (from whatever source) and a general protective function on behalf of detained patients which need not necessarily cut across the functions of MHRTs. Such a protective function might include some responsibilities in connection with the difficult problem of consent to treatment in respect of detained patients . . . . "

The Bill provides for the Mental Health Act Commission to implement this recommendation.

31. Under this provision the Secretary of State will be required to set up a special health authority to be called the Mental Health Act Commission (MHAC) to exercise a general protective function for detained patients and to carry out certain other functions given to Secretary of State in the Bill. A 'special health authority' is a body set up under the National Health Service Act 1977 and the Secretary of State makes provision for its membership, may direct it to exercise any of his powers and duties and may give it directions as to how it carries out its functions. The Commission will thus be responsible to the Secretary of State, but will be an independent body with members who will be eminent in their different fields; it will be a real safeguard to patients whereever they are detained.

32. The Government intends that the members of the proposed MHAC will be lawyers, doctors, nurses, psychologists, social workers and laymen. Their part-time services, as commissioners, will include visiting hospitals where patients are detained. There will probably be one or two visits a year to each of the 300 or so local hospitals and mental nursing homes in England and Wales

with detained patients, with around one visit a month to the four special hospitals. In their visits the Commission members will make themselves available to detained patients who wish to see them, will ensure that staff are helping patients to understand their legal position and their rights. They will look at patients' records of admission and renewal of detention and at records relating to treatment. They will also ensure that detained patients are satisfied with the handling of any complaints they may make.

33. The Commission will not trespass in any way on the Mental Health Review Tribunal's role of deciding whether an individual patient should continue to be detained; the Commission's concern will be to ensure that hospitals have adopted and are following proper procedures for using the powers of detention. The Commission will look at the use of powers, such as emergency admissions under section 29, which are outside the scope of the Tribunal. It will also have an important role in monitoring the use of the explicit power to treat detained patients without their consent subject to certain safeguards (see below): it will ensure that those safeguards are understood by staff and patients and that they are being observed.

34. Equally the proposed functions of the Commission will be separate from other inspectorial bodies; the Commission will not inspect and report on services in mental illness and mental handicap hospitals and units in the way that the Health Advisory Service and the Development Team for the Mentally Handicapped do. The Commission's concern will be the particular problems which arise from detention of specific individuals in hospital rather than the general services which affect all mentally ill and mentally handicapped patients. The name 'Mental Health Act Commission' has been chosen deliberately to emphasise its responsibilities for seeing that patients have full advantage of all the available legal safeguards under the Act as amended.

35. The Commission will have important duties concerning consent to treatment. This is currently one of the most important and most difficult issues in the mental health field and has been widely discussed. In particular there has been much debate about whether, and to what extent, staff should be authorised to impose treatment on detained patients. The Government takes the view that compulsory admission should be closely related to the prospect of benefit from treatment. It therefore proposes to provide specific statutory authority for treatment to be given to detained patients for their mental disorder without their consent in certain circumstances. But there must be safeguards for the patient and the nature of these has also been much debated. A balance must be struck between protecting the rights of the patient and providing for him to receive the treatment he needs.

36. That balance depends on the particular form of treatment. The proposals in the Bill distinguish three groups of treatment for mental disorder:—

(a) Treatments which give rise to special concern—

only to be given with the patient's consent and the agreement of an independent doctor.

(b) Other specific items of treatment prescribed under the direction of the responsible medical officer which are not identified as giving rise to special concern—

may be given without the patient's consent with the agreement of an independent doctor.

(c) Forms of treatment (including general medical and nursing care) which come within the definition of medical treatment under the Act but are not included in (a) or (b) above—

may be given without the patient's consent by or under the direction of his responsible medical officer.

Special conditions are set out for treating patients in an emergency.

37. The first group, treatments which give rise to special concern, are those where the detained patient needs most protection since (in the terms of the 1978 White Paper and the Butler Report) they are "hazardous, irreversible or not fully established". In these cases the patient's consent is needed as well as a second opinion. Paragraph 38 describes the way these treatments will be defined and paragraph 39 explains what is meant by "an independent doctor". The second group consists of specific items of treatment (such as drugs) which are not included among the treatments of special concern. The Bill will authorise the responsible medical officer to give such a treatment to a detained patient who is capable of giving consent but is unwilling to do so, provided that an independent doctor agrees that the treatment should be given. The agreement of an independent doctor to the treatment will also be necessary if a patient is unable to understand what is involved in consent to treatment. The third group includes all other treatments for mental disorder which came within the definition of "medical treatment" in the Act again excepting those which give rise to special concern. Medical treatment has a wide meaning in the Mental Health Act—it includes nursing and care, habilitation, and rehabilitation under medical supervision. The Bill provides that these treatments may be given to a detained patient without his consent, though in practice it is impossible to undertake many of the therapies concerned without a patient's co-operation.

38. The Mental Health Act Commission will have two major responsibilities in these matters. Firstly, it is intended that they will consider which treatments give rise to special concern. Some may be listed in regulations, but it will be difficult to give precise legal definitions to all the treatments which give rise to special concern and the circumstances in which they do so. For this reason the Bill provides for a Code of Practice as well as regulations. The Code will not be legally binding, but doctors would take account of it in deciding how to treat their patients. It is intended that the Mental Health Act Commission will be directed to draw up the Code of Practice, after suitable consultation, and to revise it from time to time, to take account of new and changing forms of treatment. The Code's contents will be for the Commission to decide, but it might include reference to treatments such as electroconvulsive therapy when used in particular circumstances, long acting drugs, and behaviour therapies.

39. The second major responsibility of the Mental Health Act Commission will be to appoint the "independent doctors" whose agreement must be sought. The Bill provides that agreement to treatment in the circumstances discussed

above may only be given by medical practitioners appointed for the purpose by the Secretary of State. It is intended that the Commission will exercise the Secretary of State's powers to appoint medical practitioners, who will include the psychiatrist members of the Commission itself. This will ensure that the opinions are independent and will enable the Commission both to monitor the use of the power to impose treatment and to offer advice on professional and ethical complexities. A psychiatrist so appointed who gives the second opinion on any case will be able to discuss the principles which should apply in giving second opinions with Commission members from other disciplines and to take account of their views. It is also intended that the independent doctor will discuss the patient's treatment with members of the team caring for him before giving his opinion and will take account of wider social and ethical matters. The Commission will build up considerable expertise in the care and treatment of detained patients and particularly on consent to treatment. They will be able to include in the Code of Practice and in other publications advice about all aspects of the care and treatment of detained patients and guidance on the giving of treatment for mental disorder with or without the patient's consent.

40. The Mental Health Act Commission will therefore be given important responsibilities, on behalf of the Secretary of State, on consent to treatment as well as its more general protective function for detained patients. It will also be a forum for inter-professional discussion of issues concerning the law and ethics on the treatment of detained patients. The Commission will thus have a central role in the working of the revised Mental Health Act.

CONSENT TO TREATMENT: THE PROPOSALS IN THE BILL

<table>
<tr><td>(a) Treatments which give rise to special concern
i. Listed in regulations
Must have patient's consent and agreement of independent doctor
ii. Listed in Code of Practice
Advised to have patient's consent and agreement of independent doctor</td><td rowspan="3">(d) Emergency
Treatments in (a), (b) or (c) can be given without patient's consent subject to limitations on irreversible or hazardous treatments</td></tr>
<tr><td>(b) Medication, surgery and ECT not included in (a)
Can treat without patient's consent if independent doctor agrees</td></tr>
<tr><td>(c) Other forms of treatment not included in (a) or (b)
Can treat without patient's consent</td></tr>
</table>

General: diagram applies only if —patient is detained (other than sections 29, 30, 135, 136)
—treatment is for mental disorder.

Other Safeguards

41. The Bill also proposes other changes to the law which affect detained patients in hospital. It will considerably curtail the circumstances in which incoming or outgoing mail may be withheld, and will ensure that there is no scrutiny at all of the mail of informal patients. The Bill provides that outgoing mail from a detained patient may be withheld only if the proposed recipient has asked that this should be done with correspondence addressed to him by the patient. Incoming mail will not be opened or withheld at all except in the special hospitals, where exceptional arrangements are needed for security

reasons. In the special hospitals, an officer will be authorised to withhold mail if it is necessary in the interests of the patient's safety or to protect others. This will not apply to letters from a number of persons and bodies including MPs, the Health Service Commissioner, and a Mental Health Review Tribunal. If mail is withheld from a patient in a special hospital on security grounds he will have to be informed within 24 hours and will be able to make representations to the hospital managers.

42. The proposals described above will all help staff as well as patients; one of the greatest problems in using the 1959 Act has been the uncertainty about some of its provisions. The Commission will be able to discuss, and advise on, problems concerning the law and good practice in relation to detained patients; as a result staff will benefit from clear recommendations and procedures. The proposals for handling patients' mail will also help staff in special hospitals to carry out their difficult task of caring for patients in conditions of high security. Other proposals in the Bill, notably the introduction of the nurses' holding power, will give staff clear legal protection in carrying out their professional duties.

CHAPTER 4

GUARDIANSHIP

43. A very small number of mentally disordered people who do not require treatment in hospital, either informally or formally, nevertheless need close supervision and some control in the community as a consequence of their mental disorder. These include people who are able to cope provided that they take their medication regularly, but who fail to do so, and those who neglect themselves to the point of seriously endangering their health. For such people, guardianship powers are available under section 33 of the Act. The guardian, who is usually but not always a local social services authority, is given the powers that a father has over a child under 14. These powers are therefore very wide, as well as somewhat ill-defined, and out of keeping, in their paternalistic approach, with modern attitudes to the care of the mentally disordered. The 1978 White Paper, in discussing guardianship powers in the Mental Health Act (in Chapter 4), suggested that further consideration was needed and put forward three possible options. One option was to retain guardianship powers in more or less their present form with some minor changes, eg reducing the duration of guardianship powers in line with the proposals for detention in hospital (see para 19 above). The second option was to introduce a range of community care orders to parallel existing compulsory hospital powers (the proposal of the British Association of Social Workers). The third was to introduce new specific powers to restrict the liberty of the individual only as much as is necessary to ensure that he receives medical treatment and social support and training—the "essential powers" approach.

44. The Government has considered all the issues involved and the many comments received and has decided that the third option, which was widely supported, most closely meets current needs. The Bill therefore provides that guardianship powers should be retained, but that the guardian should have only the "essential powers" rather than all the powers of the father of a child under 14 as at present. The essential powers are:—

(a) power to require the patient to live at a place specified by the guardian;
(b) power to require the patient to attend places specified by the guardian for medical treatment, occupation or training;
(c) power to ensure that a doctor, social worker or other person specified by the guardian can see the patient at his home.

The amendments proposed in the Bill mean that it will no longer be possible for patients under 16 to be received into guardianship and remove the age limit of 21 for mentally handicapped and psychopathic patients. The Bill proposes that guardianship will be required to be "in the interest of *the welfare* of the patient or for the protection of other persons" rather than "in the interests of the patient . . ." as at present; this will clarify the purpose of guardianship and ensure that the power is not so wide. Guardianship will last for 6 months initially, renewable for 6 months more, and then for a year at a time—half the present periods. This would give patients under guardianship more opportunities to apply to a Mental Health Review Tribunal (see para 26).

45. One of the effects of the proposed change in guardianship powers is that the guardian will clearly not have implicit power to consent to treatment on behalf of the patient. The proposals in the Bill for treating detained patients without their consent in certain circumstances (see paras 35–40) do not apply to patients under guardianship. Patients under guardianship will therefore be in the same position as informal (voluntary) patients where consent to treatment is concerned.

CHAPTER 5

OFFENDER PATIENTS

46. Part V of the Mental Health Act provides powers to send to hospital people who come before the courts (section 60) and people who are serving a prison sentence (section 72) and who are found to be suffering from mental disorder such as to warrant their detention in hospital. In either case, if it is felt necessary for the protection of the public, restrictions may be imposed under sections 65 or 74 respectively which mean that the person can be discharged from hospital only with the consent of the Home Secretary.

47. Many of the changes proposed for patients detained under Part IV of the Act will also apply to patients who are subject to hospital orders or transfer directions under Part V of the Act. The change in the definitions of the different forms of mental disorder will also apply in Part V. The criteria for making a hospital order are to be changed in line with the change in section 26 so that courts will not be able to make a hospital order in respect of a person suffering from psychopathic disorder or mental handicap unless there is medical evidence that medical treatment in hospital is likely to alleviate or prevent a deterioration in the offender's condition. A similar amendment will be made to the criteria on which the Home Secretary may transfer a mentally disordered prisoner to hospital. Once a patient is subject to a hospital order or transfer direction—provided he is not subject to restrictions—he benefits from all the changes proposed for Part IV patients: shorter periods of detention, more access to the Tribunal, the "benefit from treatment" test on renewal of detention, and the overall protection of the MHAC. Restricted patients too will have more opportunities to request a review by the Tribunal (see para 24) and the Commission will afford the same safeguards to restricted patients as to unrestricted patients.

48. Other proposals in the Bill apply to Part V alone. At present where a mentally disordered prisoner is transferred to hospital and made subject to a restriction order, the restrictions last until the end of his sentence, that is, until his latest date of release. Under the Bill, restrictions will be lifted on what would otherwise have been the patient's earliest date of release with remission. In response to a recommendation by the Butler Committee on Mentally Abnormal Offenders, the Bill also provides that a restriction order may only be made where it appears to the Crown Court to be necessary for the protection of the public from serious harm. At present the 1959 Act says only "necessary for the protection of the public".

49. The Bill will also implement proposals made by the Butler Committee for remands to hospital for a medical report and for treatment and for assessment to determine whether a hospital order would be a suitable method of disposal of the case. The object of these proposals is to give opportunity for a person who has been brought before the courts to be examined and treated in hospital for a limited period before a final decision is taken by the courts on his case.

50. It is proposed that remands to hospital for medical report and for treatment should last for up to 28 days, renewable for up to 12 weeks. Under the proposals remands for medical report could be made on medical evidence that there was reason to suspect that the accused person was suffering from any of the 4 categories of mental disorder; remands for treatment could only be made in cases of mental illness or severe mental handicap. In both cases remand to hospital would be considered only where bail was not possible.

51. An interim hospital order, to allow assessment of whether a hospital order would be appropriate, could be made for 12 weeks, renewable for up to 6 months, if the court were satisfied by evidence from 2 doctors that the convicted person was suffering from mental illness, psychopathic disorder, mental handicap or severe mental handicap and that a hospital order might be appropriate. An interim hospital order would be an invaluable way for the court and the hospital concerned to find out whether a hospital order is likely to be an appropriate way for the court to deal with the person. In particular, it would enable professional staff to assess whether the patient was likely to benefit from treatment.

52. The Government has recently received the judgment of the European Court of Human Rights in the case of X *v* the United Kingdom in which one of the principal issues is the question of whether or not a restricted patient has a periodic right to have the substantive grounds for his detention considered by a 'court' with power to order discharge if it finds that further detention is not justified under domestic law. Under the present law, the Home Secretary must refer the cases of restricted patients to a Tribunal periodically if they ask him to do so but the Tribunal can then only advise the Home Secretary whether to discharge the patient. It cannot itself order discharge. The Government has decided not to include in the Bill any amendments to the 1959 Act which relate to the issues in this case until the judgment of the Court has been studied. The Government will then decide whether any further amendments should be included in the Bill.

CHAPTER 6

IMPLEMENTING THE CHANGES IN THE BILL

53. Although the amendments proposed in the Bill do not alter the essential framework of the 1959 Act, they do make considerable changes in existing arrangements for the control, treatment and care of the people concerned, as well as introducing major additions to the structure, such as the Mental Health Act Commission. These changes and additions will mean new regulations, new procedures, new guidance and the provision of some extra resources of manpower and money. The introduction of these changes must therefore be carefully timed and those concerned with their practical application must be at all times clear what their legal powers are and how they must be exercised; this is especially important in matters concerning mentally disordered people where decisions may have to be taken quickly and under conditions of stress.

54. If the Bill is accepted by Parliament, it is hoped that the Royal Assent can be given in the Summer of 1982. The Government intends to bring in a Consolidation Bill soon after that. It will cover the material in the 1959 Act, as amended by subsequent legislation, including this amending legislation. The opportunity will then be taken to separate out those provisions which relate to the mentally handicapped.

55. An amending Act on the scale of that now proposed is bound to be somewhat complicated and technical as it has to be read in conjunction with the 1959 Act which it amends. The purpose of consolidation is to bring the two Acts together into a single measure which will be much easier to work with. There is therefore much to be gained by completing consolidation before the greater part of the Bill is implemented.

56. Work can start on the preparation of subordinate legislation, on the revision of advisory documents and on setting up the Mental Health Act Commission while the Consolidation Bill is being prepared. But it is impossible to be certain about the exact timing of a consolidating Bill and the Government is anxious that unforeseen delays in consolidation shall not delay implementation of these important measures. The Bill therefore specifies 30 September 1983 as the date for implementing all but three of the provisions of the Bill.

57. Some changes will be made ahead of this date in order to phase in the new programme for Mental Health Review Tribunals. During this period the Secretary of State will use his existing discretionary powers to refer to Tribunals patients who have not had a hearing for some years. He will start with those who have had the longest wait. This will reduce the backlog of hearings that will arise in the first year or so of the new scheme.

58. Certain proposals in the Bill will, however, have to be implemented separately at later dates. The obligation on social services authorities to appoint "approved social workers" will require two years preparation and training, during which the existing mental welfare officers will continue to carry out their

present functions. Health Departments will issue guidance on the new arrangements in 1982 on the standards of training, qualification and experience needed by an approved social worker and local authorities will then be able to start their work on applying guidance to their appointment and arranging for extra training and recruitment as necessary.

59. Finally, as was made clear in the 1978 White Paper, special considerations apply to the introduction of interim hospital orders and remands to hospital. Both these innovations will have some resource implications, in terms of manpower and buildings as well as money, for the NHS. They cannot be implemented until the NHS is ready to operate them. The Government therefore proposes to take powers in the Bill to introduce these—if necessary by stages—during the 2 or 3 years after the Bill is passed.

APPENDIX

TABLE 1.1: *Admission by Legal Status 1966, 1970, 1974–79.*[1] *Mental Illness and Mental Handicap Hospitals and Units in England and Wales.*[2]

SECTIONS OF THE MENTAL HEALTH ACT 1959

YEAR	25	26	29	30	60 (+65)	72	73	135	136	Other compulsory powers[3]	Total
1966	11,912	1,938	17,916	45	1,517	159	17	13	1,159	447	35,123
1970	11,143	1,214	17,260	79	1,472	117	14	11	1,485	350	33,145
1974	7,452	800	13,559	179	1,237	60	10	4	1,561	219	25,081
1975	7,196	780	12,835	206	1,278	47	13	9	1,600	217	24,181
1976	6,868	791	12,057	218	1,177	46	11	13	1,588	188	22,957
1977	6,889	836	10,257	253	1,067	60	13	9	1,516	148	21,051
1978	6,356	1,003	8,938	244	1,042	59	11	9	1,624	123	19,407
1979	6,042	1,172	8,398	299	975	89	14	10	1,623	99	18,721

[1] *Source:* Mental Health Enquiry.
[2] Figures include Special Hospitals.
[3] Other sections of the Mental Health Act 1959 or other Acts, for instance, an admission may be recorded under Section 47 of the National Assistance Act, 1948.

TABLE 1.2: *Admissions to Mental Illness Hospitals and Units in England and Wales 1966, 1970, 1974–79.*[1] *Informal and Compulsory Admissions.*[2]

	NUMBERS			PROPORTION	
YEAR	TOTAL	INFORMAL	COMPULSORY	INFORMAL	COMPULSORY
1966	170,281	136,466	33,815	80·1%	19·9%
1970	183,510	151,447	32,063	82·5%	17·5%
1974	181,451	157,015	24,436	86·5%	13·5%
1975	186,215	162,714	23,501	87·4%	12·6%
1976	190,358	168,084	22,274	88·3%	11·7%
1977	186,708	166,182	20,526	89·0%	11·0%
1978	183,372	164,487	18,885	89·7%	10·3%
1979	180,613	162,379	18,234	89·9%	10·1%

[1] *Source:* Mental Health Enquiry.
[2] Figures include Special Hospitals.

TABLE 1.3: *Admissions to Mental Handicap Hospitals and Units in England and Wales 1966, 1970, 1974–79.*[1] *Informal and Compulsory Admissions.*[2]

YEAR	TOTAL	NUMBERS		PROPORTION	
		INFORMAL	COMPULSORY	INFORMAL	COMPULSORY
1966	10,887	9,579	1,308	88·0%	12·0%
1970	11,593	10,511	1,082	90·7%	9·3%
1974	12,937	12,292	645	95·0%	5·0%
1975	13,914	13,234	680	95·1%	4·9%
1976	15,262	14,579	683	95·5%	4·5%
1977	16,170	15,645	525	96·8%	3·2%
1978	17,346	16,824	522	97·0%	3·0%
1979	18,307	17,820	487	97·3%	2·7%

[1] *Source:* Mental Health Enquiry.
[2] Numbers include Special Hospitals.

TABLE 1.4: *Admissions of Offenders under Part V 1966, 1970, 1974–79.*[1] *Mental Illness and Mental Handicap Hospitals and Units in England and Wales.*[2]

Year	SECTIONS OF THE MENTAL HEALTH ACT 1959					
	Section 60	Section 60 with Section 65	Section 72	Section 72 with Section 74	Section 73 with Section 74	TOTAL
1966	1,259	181	16	133	16	1,605
1970	1,039	278	18	89	17	1,441
1974	808	196	4	40	12	1,060
1975	861	156	5	39	15	1,076
1976	773	151	6	37	13	980
1977	731	90	11	45	18	895
1978	682	127	12	41	9	871
1979	657	102	14	70	16	859

[1] *Source:* Home Office Criminal Statistics for England and Wales.
[2] Figures include Special Hospitals.

TABLE 2.1: *Residents by Legal Status at 31 December 1974–79.*[1] *Mental Illness and Mental Handicap Hospitals and Units in England and Wales.*[3]

YEAR	SECTIONS OF THE MENTAL HEALTH ACT 1959 25	26	29	30	60(+65), 61	71(2) 72+73	135+136	Other[4] compulsory powers	TOTAL
1974	1,107	2,834	128	20	2,734	251	23	796	7,893
1975	1,272	2,717	102	16	2,673	257	4	639	7,680
1976	985	2,725	101	22	2,595	251	9	580	7,268
1977	860	2,885	94	16	2,496	249	10	487	7,097
1978	878	2,976	103	21	2,350	236	24	445	7,033
1979	908	3,175	99	24	2,327	232	16	391	7,172

[1] Figures for previous years are not comparable as the method of collection was revised for 1974.
[2] *Source:* Form SBH 13C.
[3] Figures include Special Hospitals.
[4] Other sections of the Mental Health Act 1959 or other Acts, for instance, an admission may be recorded under section 47 of the National Assistance Act, 1948.

TABLE 2.2: *Residents in Mental Illness and Mental Handicap Hospitals and Units in England and Wales*[3] *at 31 December 1974–79.*[1]

YEAR	NUMBERS TOTAL	INFORMAL	COMPULSORY	PROPORTION INFORMAL	COMPULSORY
1974	150,857	142,964	7,893	94·8%	5·2%
1975	146,718	139,038	7,680	94·8%	5·2%
1976	142,272	135,004	7,268	94·9%	5·1%
1977	138,438	131,341	7,097	94·9%	5·1%
1978	134,618	127,585	7,033	94·8%	5·2%
1979	131,095	123,923	7,172	94·5%	5·5%

[1] Figures for previous years are not comparable as the method of collection was revised for 1974.
[2] *Source:* SBH 13C.
[3] Figures include Special Hospitals.

TABLE 3: *Use of Guardianship Powers Under Sections 33 and 60 for Mentally Ill and Mentally Handicapped People in England and Wales, 1966, 1970, 1974–78.*[2]

Date	Mentally ill[4]	Mentally handicapped[5]	Total[3]
21 December 1966	17	302	319 (9)
31 December 1970	21	207	228 (5)
31 March 1974	26	200	226 (7)
31 March 1975	27	141	168 (4)
31 March 1976	33	144	177 (4)
31 March 1977	32	144	176 (4)
31 March 1978	37	101	138 (8)

1 *Source:* SSDA 702 and Home Office Criminal Statistics.
2 Figures for 1979 not available.
3 Figures in parentheses are the numbers of guardianship orders under Section 60 in each year.
4 Includes psychopathic disorder.
5 Includes severely mentally handicapped.
6 Figures in Cmnd 7320 have been amended.

TABLE 3.1: *Resident Patients by Mental Category at 31 December 1974–79.*[1] *Mental Illness and Mental Handicap Hospitals and Units in England and Wales.*[2]

Year		Mental Illness	Psychopathic Disorder	Mental Handicap	Severe Mental Handicap	Other	All
1974	Informal	89,418	582	12,289	39,746	929	142,964
	Compulsory	5,174	807	1,059	807	46	7,893
	All	94,592	1,389	13,348	40,553	975	150,857
1975	Informal	85,818	564	12,581	38,984	1,091	139,038
	Compulsory	4,899	787	964	976	54	7,680
	All	90,717	1,351	13,545	39,960	1,145	146,718
1976	Informal	84,660	470	10,948	37,838	1,088	135,004
	Compulsory	4,906	760	827	711	64	7,268
	All	89,566	1,230	11,774	38,549	1,152	142,272
1977	Informal	80,035	513	11,265	38,337	1,191	131,341
	Compulsory	4,936	721	770	608	62	7,097
	All	84,971	1,234	12,035	38,945	1,253	138,438
1978	Informal	77,253	484	10,891	37,709	1,248	127,585
	Compulsory	5,022	696	709	545	61	7,033
	All	82,275	1,180	11,600	38,255	1,308	134,618
1979	Informal	75,249	423	10,239	36,887	1,125	123,923
	Compulsory	5,295	638	685	484	70	7,172
	All	80,544	1,061	10.924	37,371	1,195	131,095

[1] *Source:* Form SBH 13C.
[2] Figures include Special Hospitals.

Printed in England for Her Majesty's Stationery Office by Oyez Press Limited
Dd 294663 C40 11/81

HER MAJESTY'S STATIONERY OFFICE

Government Bookshops

49 High Holborn, London WC1V 6HB
13a Castle Street, Edinburgh EH2 3AR
41 The Hayes, Cardiff CF1 1JW
Brazennose Street, Manchester M60 8AS
Southey House, Wine Street, Bristol BS1 2BQ
258 Broad Street, Birmingham B1 2HE
80 Chichester Street, Belfast BT1 4JY

Government publications are also available through booksellers

ISBN 0 10 184050 0